In Love & Revolution

Anna Akhmatova

In Love & Revolution
—*Selected Poems*—

translated from the Russian by
Stephen Capus

Shearsman Books

First published in the United Kingdom in 2025 by
Shearsman Books Ltd
PO Box 4239
Swindon
SN3 9FN

Shearsman Books Ltd Registered Office
30–31 St. James Place, Mangotsfield, Bristol BS16 9JB
(this address not for correspondence)

www.shearsman.com

ISBN 978-1-84861-968-5

Introduction and translations
copyright © Stephen Capus, 2025

The right of Stephen Capus to be identified as the translator of this work has been asserted by him in accordance with the Copyrights, Designs and Patents Act of 1988.
All rights reserved.

ACKNOWLEDGEMENTS
are due to the following periodicals in which some of these translations have previously appeared: *Acumen, Cardinal Points, Los Angeles Review of Books* and *Shearsman*.

Contents

Introduction   9

from *EVENING* (1912)

A half-open door   17
'Why so pale tonight?' you enquired   18
Silvery-grey, high above in the sky   19
Though my breast grew hopelessly colder   20
from In Tsarskoe Selo   21
Love   22
from Deception   23
Masquerade in the Park   24
The King with Grey Eyes   25
Three Things…   26
They haven't brought any letters for me today   27
Imitation of I.F. Annensky   28

from *ROSARY* (1914)

Evening   31
Here we're all whores and carousers   32
We walked along the embankment for one last time   33
From your desk do you hear a rustle   34
The Voice of Memory   35
8 November 1913   36
Beneath the icon the carpet is worn; the frame   37
I came to visit the poet   38

from *WHITE FLOCK* (1917)

Alone in this frozen house I no longer   41
Bright yellow lamps, a shadowy road   42
God shows no mercy to reapers and gardeners   43
Snow   44
July 1914   45

Solace	47
Prayer	48
In Memory of 19th July 1914	49
I'll draw out from the depths of your memory a far-off day	50
The twenty first. At night. On a Monday.	51

from *PLANTAIN* (1921)

When on his far-away island he comes to learn	55
In the course of each day a certain	56
What makes this age so much worse than any other?	57

from *ANNO DOMINI MCMXXI* (1921–1922)

I wasn't one of those who abandoned my country	61
from Biblical Verses	62
As the mornings grow colder it's good to hear	63
Everything's squandered, pillaged and plundered,	64
Today is the feast of Our Lady	65
Three Poems	66
New Year's Ballad	67

from REED (1924–1940)

The Muse	71
Voronezh	72
Dante	73
Wild honey smells of freedom, the scent	74
The Willow	75
When someone dies all his portraits	76
Thus sombre souls take wing and wander	77
Mayakovsky in 1913	78

from SEVENTH BOOK (1936–1964)

from Craft Secrets	81
from In the Year 1940	83
from The Wind of War	84
from Three Poems	86
Sketches from Komarovo	87
from Poem Without a Hero	88
Requiem	92
Notes	102

*In memory of my mother and father,
with love and gratitude.*

Introduction

Anna Akhmatova was born near Odesa in 1889. Christened as Anna Gorenko, she adopted her pen-name from the family of her mother. She attended school in Tsarskoe Selo and lived most of her life in Saint Petersburg, the city with which so much of her poetry is intimately connected. She frequented the Tower, the famous literary salon of the symbolist poet Vyacheslav Ivanov, and in 1910 she married fellow poet Nikolay Gumilev. Together they became associated with the literary movement known as Acmeism. The couple were divorced in 1918, three years before Gumilev was executed by the Bolsheviks for counter-revolutionary activities.

Akhmatova achieved fame with her first collection of poems, *Evening*, published in 1912, and her subsequent collections, *Rosary* and *White Flock*, consolidated her reputation as one of Russia's leading poets during the period preceding the October Revolution. After 1917 she took the decision to remain in Russia, rather than join those of her fellow writers who were opting to go into exile in the West. Between the publication of the second edition of *Anno Domini* in 1923 and the death of Stalin in 1953—with a brief reprieve during the Great Patriotic War—she found herself subject to censorship, and in 1946 she was expelled from the Soviet Writers' Union in the wake of the notorious speech by the Communist Party cultural boss Andrey Zhdanov, in which he described her as a 'cross between a nun and a whore'. Nonetheless, although she faced much personal hardship and a protracted exclusion from publication as a consequence of her decision to remain in Russia, she was also able to create *Requiem*, her great affirmation of solidarity with the victims of the Stalinist purges.

After Stalin's death in 1953 the restrictions on Akhmatova's work were gradually relaxed and a selection of her poems, entitled *The Course of Time*, was published in 1958. She died in Moscow in 1966, and in 1976 a more comprehensive selection of her poetry was published in the prestigious Poet's Library series.

Akhmatova's early collections of poetry reflect the values of the Russian literary group known as Acmeism, which was founded in reaction to the dominant movement of *fin-de-siècle* Russian poetry, Symbolism, and which advocated the virtues of craftsmanship, reticence and clarity. Her poems written before World War 1 are concerned above all with personal themes, including the disappointments—and occasionally the joys—of romantic love, and show a predilection for the use of concrete imagery to allude obliquely to complex emotional states. With the publication of *White Flock* in 1917 she broadened her range to include themes of war and social upheaval, a trend which reached its culmination in the cycle *Requiem*. The translations included in this selection are intended to illustrate Akhmatova's progress over the course of her literary career from a poet of private experience to the public witness of the collective traumas and travails of the Russian people who emerges in her later works.

The literary culture in which Akhmatova published her earliest poems was one which attached a high value to formal qualities and which, for all its thematic and technical innovation, continued to draw on the traditions of the preceding century. Akhmatova was, then, the product of an aesthetic culture whose assumptions were very different from those which govern English-Language poetry in the early 21st century; and although in her writings she was to question and expand the poetic practices of her time, she always remained a Russian poet whose sensibility was shaped in the early 20th century.

The difference of her work, the alternative idea of poetry which it is able to offer, constitutes one its fascinations for a contemporary British or American reader. In my opinion, therefore, she should be permitted to retain her difference in translation. This point needs to be emphasized as there is a tendency apparent in the translation of foreign poetry to elide the strangeness of the original poem under the pretext of naturalization—to assist the foreign text to accommodate itself to the English language by compelling it to reflect contemporary English-language poetic taste. Clearly, one of the tasks of the translator is indeed to help the foreign poem feel at home in the English language, to enable it to read like a poem in English, rather than a translation. But this process of naturalization doesn't have to be understood—as it sometimes is in contemporary translation practice—as an exercise in constraining the original text to conform to the aesthetic orthodoxies of contemporary English-Language poetry. As I've suggested, if there are reasons for reading poetry in translation, one of these is surely to enable the reader to encounter different conceptions of what poetry can be.

Translation, rather than making a foreign poem sound reassuringly familiar to the reader, should challenge the reader's assumptions as to what constitutes a good poem. It is therefore surely a mistake to require a poet like Akhmatova to sound in translation like a competent, if rather dull, contemporary English-language poet. The aesthetic rules of contemporary English-language poetry are just that—a set of particular criteria, for the most part tacitly assumed, defining what constitutes a good poem; and these criteria have in turn been heavily influenced by the positivist, pragmatic, commonsensical values which dominate the general culture of the contemporary English speaking world. What they are not is a set of universal prescriptions to which all poetry from all countries and eras must conform if it is to have any value.

Anna Akhmatova was a formal poet—her poems are characterized by regular metrical and rhyming patterns, as well as a high degree of syntactic and semantic parallelism—and if the distinctiveness of her work is to be preserved, these qualities must be conveyed in translation—not least because they play a central role in the construction of meaning.

Poetry, like prose, can develop linear arguments, tell stories and describe people and places. But it also constructs meaning in an another way, one which the Russian critic Roman Jakobson has argued is characteristic of poetry as an art form. In the view of Jakobson and his structuralist followers, poetry not only unfolds meaning progressively, along the horizontal axis of the text, but it also constructs meaning along the vertical axis of the text, through the elaboration of semantic, syntactic and phonic patterns based on relations of similarity and contrast. And in the poetry of Akhmatova, as in that of other major Russian poets of the early 20th century, an important role in the composition of these synchronic patterns is played by rhyme and formal meter. Semantic structures based on repetition and contrast interact with, and are enhanced by, patterns of syntax and sound which include rhyme and meter. In the poetry of Akhmatova, rhyme and meter, far from playing a merely decorative role, are integral to the construction of meaning.

The translator who resolves to reproduce the formal meters of Russian poetry will obviously have to contend with a number of problems which stem from the objective differences between the Russian and English languages. Among these are the absence of secondary stresses in polysyllabic Russian words, as a result of which the formal Russian meters naturally display a greater degree of rhythmic variety than do their English equivalents; and the highly inflected nature of the Russian language, which produces a greater abundance of exact rhymes than is available in English.

Something of the rhythmic variety which characterizes the classic formal meters in Russian can be recaptured through the use in translation of a hybrid binary/ternary meter in which the number of stressed syllables in each line remains constant, while the intervals of unstressed syllables vary from one to two. This meter, which was known as a *dol'nik* in traditional Russian prosody and is often employed by Akhmatova, enables the translator to reproduce the effects of the classic Russian binary and ternary meters, while at the same time preserving a degree of rhythmic variation. Alongside these hybrid patterns, the more regular binary and ternary meters have also been employed where they've seemed to be more appropriate.

The greater availability of exact rhymes in Russian, as compared with English, certainly presents the translator with a formidable challenge. However, if the notion of rhyme is expanded to include assonance, compound rhyme etc., English can turn out to be more richly endowed than is sometimes supposed. The use of assonance is particularly appropriate in the translation of Akhmatova, as it's a variety of rhyme whose expressive potential she herself explored with great sensitivity and resourcefulness in her poetry.

Various arguments have been forwarded against the reproduction of formal meters and rhyme in poetry translation—or for that matter against their use in English poetry generally. A frequently encountered argument is that the classical formal meters have long since become worn out and stale through over-familiarity. However, such an argument surely involves a misrepresentation of the way in which formal meters are actually experienced by the reader. For the reader experiences formal meter, not as a pure, naked, abstract pattern of stressed and unstressed syllables, but rather as embodied in an actual, particular poem, where it interacts with and is informed by all the other elements of which the poem is composed: with its syntactic and phonetic structure, its lexicon, stylistic register, rhyme-scheme and subject matter. And each time a formal meter is embodied in the concrete reality of an individual poem, the abstract pattern is refreshed and revitalized. The iambic pentameter as embodied in Milton's *Paradise Lost*—with its systematic use of enjambment—is not quite the same meter which we find in Pope's *Rape of the Lock*—where the metrical and syntactic units tend to coincide; nor is the iambic tetrameter we find in Wordsworth's 'I wandered lonely as a cloud…' identical with the iambic tetrameter of Larkin's 'This be the Verse'—where the familiar meter is clothed in, and coloured by, an unexpectedly colloquial, if not downright profane, stylistic register. The classical meters can never quite be exhausted because they're endlessly renewed each time they're embodied in the fresh context of a creatively original poem.

Of course, all verse forms are susceptible to overfamiliarity, while being equally capable of renewal and revitalization. However, it's a mistake to assume that the risk of overfamiliarity is unique to the classic meters, and can therefore be avoided simply by opting to discard them in favour of free verse or accentual verse (in which the number of stressed syllables remains constant while the intervals of unstressed syllables are variable). For this assumption rests on the erroneous belief that free verse and accentual verse are not themselves conventional verse forms—which is what they in fact are: formal choices which are all the more likely to be experienced as stale and worn due to their ubiquity in contemporary English-language poetry.

A more general cultural argument which is sometimes urged against the retention of meter and rhyme in the translation of poetry is that formal regularity is somehow alien to the essential character of the English language. The language, like the people, it is argued, is essentially freedom-loving and naturally chafes against the kind of rules and regulations which are tolerated by less enlightened cultures. And yet the claim that English possesses some kind of essential character which is inimical to formal prosodic patterns surely involves a misunderstanding of the nature of language, whether English or any other. For although a language at a given moment will obviously display certain objective features of the kind discussed above, it possesses no ahistorical, inalienable essence or soul. On the contrary, such character(s) as English possesses are the product of its long and contested history, and as such these historically produced characteristics are always open to further development. As has been argued by the Russian critic Mikhail Bakhtin, the natural condition of language is heterogeneity. There is no one English language possessing a single, pure, fixed essence, but rather a plurality of English-es, incorporating the varying perspectives and aspirations of the of the different social groups which have engaged with the language in the course of history.

English, then, is endlessly open and adaptable, and whatever the prejudices and habits by which it is dominated at a given historical moment, it is always capable of growing and expanding to accommodate new approaches to the writing of poetry. The translations which follow, therefore, won't attempt to disguise what might appear to be the 'alien, un-English' quality of Akhmatova's poetry. Above all, they'll endeavour to capture the interaction and mutual enrichment of form and meaning which lends her poems such power. It is hoped that they will thereby enable the English-speaking reader to acquire a notion, however imperfect, of the aesthetic experience of reading the poems of Anna Akhmatova in Russian.

from: EVENING (1912)

La Fleur des vignes pousse
Et j'ai vingt ans ce soir.

    André Theuriet

* * *

A half-open door,
On a table top,
A forgotten glove
And a riding crop.

Lamp-light, the rustle
Of limes in the breeze;
I search for an answer
—Why did you leave?

A clear dawn tomorrow
Will gladden the sky;
Life is so beautiful,
Heart, now be wise.

You're tired and the turmoil
Subsides by and by;
I recall reading somewhere
The soul never dies.

17th February 1911
Tsarskoe Selo

* * *

'Why so pale tonight?' you enquired.
I clasped my hands beneath
My veil. 'It's because I've made him
Drunk on astringent grief.'

Will I ever forget? He was swaying
As he got up to leave and his mouth
Was contorted with anguish. I flew down
The stairs and followed him out.

Breathless, I cried: 'It was only
A joke. I'll die if you go.'
And he said to me, smiling so calmly,
So strangely: 'Take care, you'll catch cold.'

8 January 1911
Kiev

* * *

Silvery-grey, high above in the sky,
A cloud was spread out like a squirrel's pelt;
He said: 'Why should I care, my fragile Snow Maiden,
If March has arrived and you're starting to melt?'

A feeling of terror, confusion, seized me,
In my opulent muff my hands grew colder;
How can I make them return, the swift weeks
Of a love so brief it's already over?

Let me die in the midst of the final snow-storm,
It's hard to endure such pain for us both;
He appeared in a dream on the Feast of the Epiphany;
By the end of the month we'd already grown close.

Spring 1911
Tsarskoe Selo

* * *

Though my breast grew hopelessly colder,
My steps were rapid and light;
Distracted, I pulled on my left hand
The glove which belonged on the right.

The steps of the staircase seemed endless
—Though I knew there were only three!
Through the maples a voice in autumn
Whispered: 'Come die with me!

All my life I've been dogged by a morbid
And volatile fate.' I replied:
'My darling, misfortune's pursued me
As well—let me die by your side!'

The song of final meeting
Has ended. I gazed upon
The dark house. In the bedroom a candle,
Indifferently yellow, still shone.

29 September 1911
Tsarskoe Selo

from In Tsarskoe Selo

1

As the horses are led along shady alleys
Their neatly combed manes are like rippling streams;
It makes me sad to love you so much,
Oh, enchanting city of mysteries and dreams.

And it's strange to remember: my heart was in anguish,
I struggled for breath, on the edge of despair;
But now, like my friend, the pink cockatoo,
I've become a child's plaything, a stranger to care.

If you want you can gaze in my eyes—this isn't
A portent of pain which my heart has disclosed.
All I dislike is the wind from the sea,
The hour before dusk and the little word 'go'.

22 February 1911
Tsarskoe Selo

Love

Coiled up in your heart like a serpent,
It casts its seductive spell;
On White Nights you can hear how it coos,
Like a dove, from your window sill.

It might drowse in a daisy's petals,
Or appear in the gleam of the frost;
But you know it will secretly lead you
To a place where all peace will be lost.

It knows how to sob so sweetly
In the sad violin, like a prayer;
And to guess that it's there in the smile
Of a stranger can fill you with fear.

24 November 1911
Tsarskoe Selo

from Deception

1
M.A. Zmunchilla

The morning is drunk with dazzling Spring weather,
Through the terrace a perfume of roses drifts
And the sky is as bright as a vase of blue porcelain.
In a notebook bound in Morocco leather,
Soft and red, I read elegant quatrains,
Composed for my grandmother once as a gift.

I follow the path to the gate as it winds
Across emerald green lawns, between orderly rows
Of white posts. Oh, love is so sweet, and yet blind!
Motley flower-beds enliven the park,
The night is disturbed by the cawing of crows
And the arch of the crypt yawns wide in the dark.

2 November 1910
Kiev

Masquerade in the Park

Moonlight glimmered on cornices
And gleamed on the rippling crests
Of the river. How fragrant and cold
Are hands of the masked marchioness.

'Oh, prince,' she laughed as she curtsied,
'You're my partner tonight in the dance.'
And behind her mask she grew paler
From forebodings of stormy romance.

Branches of poplar obscured
The porch with a silvery veil.
'For you I'll capture Baghdad or
Constantinople, *ma belle*!'

'Marchioness, I'm afraid to embrace you,
So rarely you smile—if at all'
The arbour was cool and shady.
'And now, shall we go to the ball?'

They go out where the trees are festooned with
Coloured lanterns which hang from their trunks
And two ladies in green satin dresses
Are playing cards with two monks.

And they're met by Pierrot, pale and smiling,
With a scented bouquet: 'Let me guess,
My prince: was it you stole a feather
From the hat of our sweet marchioness?'

1912

The King with Grey Eyes

Hail, infinite grief! The king with grey eyes
Is dead, but my sorrow will never subside.

Autumn glowed red as the evening grew dark;
My husband came home and calmly remarked:

'He'd gone out to hunt by himself all day;
He was found beneath the old oak tree, they say.

I pity the queen: in the space of one night,
Although she's so young, her hair has turned white!'

From above the fire-place he took down his pipe
And went off to the work which detains him each night.

And now I must wake my child right away
And gaze at her beautiful eyes of grey;

While through the window the poplars sing:
'The earth is no longer home to your king…'

11 September 1910
Tsarskoe Selo

Three Things…

Three things he loved more than anything in
The world: white peacocks, maps of America,
Old and faded, the singing of hymns
At vespers… He hated female hysterics
And children in tears, nor did he like
Raspberry tea… And I was his wife.

9 November 1910
Kiev

* * *

They haven't brought any letters for me today:
Perhaps he's already left, or forgotten to write.
Spring is like warbling laughter, silvery bright;
The idle ships are rocking out in the bay.
They haven't brought any letters for me today.

Not long ago he still was by my side;
He seemed so sweet, so much in love, so mine;
But that was in the snow-white winter time;
Now Spring has come, its sadness makes me cry.
Not long ago he still was by my side.

I listen: the sad violin is tremulous, light,
As it sings of approaching death. My heart is aching
So much I begin to fear it might be breaking.
These lines are almost more than I can write.

1912

Imitation of I.F. Annensky

First of my many caprices,
When we parted the East glimmered blue;
All you said was: 'I'll love you forever.'
But I doubted your words could be true.

First we love one, then another
As faces and years come and go;
Once I turned down this page at the corner
—Why, I no longer know.

And always the book falls open
At the very same page—it's so strange!
All I love is the blue of chrysanthemums
And the joy which lasts for a day.

The heart's surely made of fire
Though some claim it consists of stone…
But whether you only loved me,
Or were close to me then—who knows?

1911

from *ROSARY* (1914)

Then bid farewell forever, and yet know
That in my poems of love you'll find the names
Of not just one, but two, who are to blame.

        Baratynsky

Evening

The sound of music filled the garden
With a sorrow too deep to be shared;
From a dish of oysters on ice the scent
Of the sea pervaded the air.

He said: 'I'm your faithful friend forever!'
And his fingers brushed my dress;
How little it felt like a lover's embrace—
The glance of his gentle caress.

This is how men stroke a cat or admire
A horsewoman riding by;
Beneath golden lashes a hint of mockery
Gleamed in his cold, calm eyes.

Through drifting mist a sad violin
Sang out from somewhere far off;
'Give thanks to heaven—for the very first time
You're alone with the one you love.'

March 1913

* * *

Here we're all whores and carousers,
How sadly together we crowd;
On the walls there are painted flowers
And birds which yearn for the clouds.

The smoke from your cigarette sketches
Strange shapes in the air above;
The skirt which I wear is close-fitting
For tonight I long to be loved.

Sealed windows shut out the weather—
Is it hoarfrost or storm outside?
A delicate feline caution
Seems to show in the light of your eyes.

Is this angst in my heart a sign that
The end is close? Who can tell?
But that girl who dances is surely
Destined to end up in hell.

1 January 1913

* * *

We walked along the embankment for one last time,
Where often in the past we'd walked together;
The Neva's turbulent waters swirled close by;
In town they feared floods and stormy weather.

He spoke of summer and then went on to say
A female poet makes no sense whatever;
The majestic sight of the Winter Palace that day
Impressed itself on my memory forever.

For the light that bathed the city wasn't ours
But seemed instead like a gift from high above;
And I knew that I was granted in that hour
The chance of one last wayward song of love.

January 1914

* * *

From your desk do you hear a rustle
Announcing that I've come?
And now it's too late to finish
The line you've just begun.
Surely you won't offend me
As you did when I last came by
—But you say that you notice nothing,
Neither my hands nor my eyes.
Life with you is clear and simple—
Please don't drive me now to go
Where beneath the bridge the river's
Turbid waters flow.

October 1913

The Voice of Memory

To O.A. Glebova-Sudeykina

What do you see as the tardy dawn climbs the sky
And you gaze at the vacant wall with your lustreless eyes?

Is it a seagull, adrift on a deep blue sea
—Or the Boboli Gardens in Florence, perhaps, which you see?

Or do you remember the royal park on the day
You followed the path where anxiety stood in your way?

Or do you see the one who has found release
From your thrall in death, clinging still to your knees?

No, all I see is a wall—and on it, the rays
Of the sun, reflected and slowly dying away.

18 June 1913
Slepnevo

8 November 1913

Dawn filled the room with slanting
Sunbeams, quick with the play
Of dust motes; I woke and remembered
It's your name-day, my darling, today.
That's why through the window the snow-drifts
Are warmed by a wintery light;
That's why, like a novice communicant,
I've lain wide awake all night.

* * *

Beneath the icon the carpet is worn; the frame
Of the spacious window is all enmeshed
In densely woven clusters of dark green ivy;
The light is dim, the air is fresh.

A delicate scent of roses gently circulates,
The lamp near the icon fitfully shines;
The loving hands of the craftsman have covered the chest
In a colourful web of ingenious designs.

An embroidery frame shows white beneath the window…
Stern thoughts can be read in your profiled face;
Concealing the hand he smothered in passionate kisses
Beneath your shawl, you betray your distaste.

And your heart has started to beat with a frightening violence;
Already your troubled breast is filled
With such anguish; and in those slightly disordered tresses
A hint of tobacco smoke lingers still.

1912

* * *

To Aleksandr Blok

I came to visit the poet
At 12 o'clock. On a Sunday.
The spacious room was quiet,
Through the window gleamed the frost

And a crimson sun was floating
Above waves of dishevelled blue mist.
How clear was the gaze of my taciturn
Host as he looked at me!

No one could ever forget
Those eyes of his—though I
Decided it's best to be cautious
And avoid their look altogether.

But still I remember our talk
And the mist, at noon, on a Sunday,
And that building, austere and lofty,
Where the Neva flows back to the sea.

January 1914

from *WHITE FLOCK* (1917)

Even at night for grief the way is clear.

—Annensky

* * *

Alone in this frozen house I no longer
Count the long days, so deathly calm;
The Epistles of Paul are all I now read,
All I now read are King David's Psalms.
But the stars still shine blue and the snow is deep,
New encounters occur every day;
When I search in my bible for Solomon's Song,
A maple leaf still marks the page.

Winter 1915

* * *

Bright yellow lamps, a shadowy road
Which leads to the park by the sea.
Today I'm quite calm; all I ask is: please,
Don't mention his name to me.
You're faithful, you're sweet—I'm sure we'll be friends,
We'll stroll, exchange kisses, turn grey…
And above us, like stars of snow, the swift months
Will glimmer and hurry away.

March 1914

* * *

God shows no mercy to reapers and gardeners:
Murmuring rains streak the sky, and the lake,
Reflecting the clouds high above, is festooned
With a motley riot of capes.

Meadows and fields are submerged in a watery
Realm as the deluge hums through the sky;
On swollen branches plums are ripening,
The mown grass decays where it lies.

And through a thick veil of insistent rain
I glimpse your dear face once more,
The quiet park, the Chinese pavilion
And a house, its round porch and front door.

Summer 1915
Tsarskoe Selo

Snow

A transparent shroud covers the grass
Then melts away. The cruel
Cold of spring destroys the buds
As they ripen. It's hard to endure
The sight of so many early deaths
All over God's world. King David
Bequeathed this sorrow that fills my heart
Like a royal gift to the ages.

1916
Slepnevo

July 1914

1

A smell of burning. The peat-bogs have blazed
For a month now without reprieve.
Even the birds are silent today,
Not a breath stirs the aspen's leaves.

The sun looms above like a sign of God's anger,
The crops have thirsted for rain
Since Easter. One day a stranger on crutches
Entered the yard and proclaimed:

'An age of terror will soon be coming,
The earth will be strewn with the dead;
Beware of earthquakes, plague and famine
As the sky grows dark overhead.

But in vain the cruel foe will covet
Our land—his designs will fail;
The Mother of God in her mercy will cover
Our grief with a pure white veil.'

2

A scent of juniper berries
Drifts from a forest in flame;
In the village soldiers' wives weep for
Their children and widows complain.

The earth, long deprived of rainfall,
Needed those prayers which were said:
The only moisture these trampled
Fields have been granted is red.

The desolate sky sinks lower,
And this quiet lament can be heard:

'They cast lots for a share of your garments
And wound your flesh with their swords.'

20 July 1914

Solace

*And there the Archangel Michael
Counts him among his host.*
    —N Gumilev

You'll never find the place where he's buried
In sorrowful Poland, scorched by flame;
You'll never learn of his fate in a letter,
You'll never see him again.

But let your mind remain calm and tranquil;
There's nothing more to fear:
A new recruit to the heavenly army,
What need does he have of tears?

To weep is a sin, to grieve in the peace of
Your family home is a sin;
Just think: you've gained a protector in heaven,
From now on you can pray to him.

*September 1914
Tsarskoe Selo*

Prayer

Torment me with years of sickness,
Deprive me of sleep and of breath,
Deny me the gift of poetry,
Take my friend, take my child from my breast—
I offered this prayer during matins,
After so many troubled days,
That the storm clouds which hang over Russia
Might be pierced by the sun's glorious rays.

May 1915. Whit Monday.
Petersburg

In Memory of 19th July 1914

It seemed we'd grown a hundred years older,
Then in just one hour it came to this:
Already the fleeting summer was over,
The freshly ploughed fields were covered in mist.

All at once the roads were motley with colour,
From every direction came ringing laments;
And covering my face, I begged the Almighty
To kill me before the first battles commence.

Like superfluous clutter expelled from my memory,
The shades of passions and poems all fled;
And God bade my vacant soul become the
Record of terrible tidings instead.

Summer 1916
Slepnevo

***

I'll draw out from the depths of your memory a far-off day
And prompt your mist-blurred gaze to inquire once more:
That spray of Persian lilac, those swallows in flight,
That small wooden house—where have I seen them before?

How often in future days you'll suddenly remember
The sadness of nameless longings, confused, inexact,
And, pensively roaming the city, you'll try to find
That street which isn't included in any map!

Hearing the sound of a voice through a half-open window,
Catching sight of a letter that's come in the post,
You'll silently say to yourself: 'She's here once more,
She's come to help me retrieve the faith which I've lost.

4 April 1915

* * *

The twenty first. At night. On a Monday.
The city's outline dissolves in the mist.
Some idiot once claimed that on this earth
Love now and then really does exist.

And from idleness, maybe, or else out of boredom,
Most people live as if he were right:
They make assignations and dread separation
And sing about love, its pain and delight.

But to some the secret has been disclosed
And they gradually all grow still…
I stumbled upon it quite by chance
And since then it's as if I've been ill.

1917
Petersburg

from *PLANTAIN* (1921)

And recognize the sounds which once,
At least, were dear to you.

    Pushkin

* * *

When on his far-away island he comes to learn
The news of my bitter death, whether sooner or later,
He won't be sad, nor will he grow more stern,
But smiling wryly, he'll turn a little paler.
And then he'll recall the winter sky once more
And the blizzard swirling along the banks of the Neva;
And then he'll recall how once he solemnly swore
He'd always be there to protect his Russian lover.

1917

* * *

In the course of each day a certain
Troubling hour arrives
When I start to converse with sorrow
Out loud, before opening my eyes.
This sorrow of mine is as warm
As breath, it beats like the blood
In my veins. It's as cunning and cruel
As a happy, contented love.

1917

* * *

What makes this age so much worse than any other?
Perhaps it's this: that amongst all these muddled alarms
And tears, it's exposed itself to a kind of damage
For which it can find no balm.

And now in the west the day is already declining,
The city's roof-tops are glimmering in the sun,
And, marking each house with a cross, death's pallid angel
Summons the ravens, and at her call they come.

Winter 1919

from *ANNO DOMINI MCMXXI* (1921–1922)

In those legendary years…

Tyutchev

* * *

I wasn't one of those who abandoned my country,
Who left her to be dismembered by her foes;
To me their vulgar flattery means nothing,
It isn't for them my poems are composed.

But I grieve for the captive, the sick, and can still feel pity
For those who, cast out by their native land, have fled
To safety: dark is the road you travel, wanderer,
And bitter is the taste of alien bread.

And here, allowing the little which remains of
Our youth to perish in flames and blinding smoke,
We always stood prepared to face the onslaught
Nor did we try to evade a single stroke.

And we know each hour of our lives will be approved by
Posterity's final verdict after we've died…
For nowhere in all the world was anyone ever
More honest than us, more proud, or more clear-eyed.

July 1922
Petersburg

from Biblical Verses

    2

Lot's Wife

> *But behind him Lot's wife turned to look and became*
> *a pillar of salt.*
> —The Book of Genesis

And the one righteous man followed God's messenger,
Radiant and tall, up the lowering hill;
But his wife was disturbed by a nagging temptation:
Is it too late—or could she not still

Behold the lofty red towers of Sodom,
Her city, the yard where she worked, the square
Where she sang, and the house with its empty windows
Which she and her husband and children once shared.

So she turned to look—but her eyes could no longer
See through the pain by which they were bound;
And her body became a transparent column
Of salt, and her limbs were fixed to the ground.

Why should we weep for Lot's wife—she was surely
The least of the losses suffered that day?
Yet my heart can't forget that for one last glance
She was ready to throw her whole life away.

24 February 1924

* * *

As the mornings grow colder it's good to hear
The crackle and rustle of winter all round;
In a burst of white flame an icily dazzling
Cluster of roses bows down to the ground.
And there in the opulent snow which covers
The pavement someone on skis has traced
A line which reminds me that once you and I
Walked side by side in this very same place.

1922

* * *

To Natalya Rykova

Everything's squandered, pillaged and plundered,
Death's black wing has swept through the night;
Everything's swallowed by ravenous anguish
—Then why has it now turned suddenly bright?

All day, near the town, the forest is wafting
The perfume of cherry trees far and wide;
All night long new constellations
Gleam deep in the limpid skies of July.

And closer and closer the marvel approaches
These ramshackle houses, all covered in grime…
And nobody knows it, no one at all
—Yet it's what we've wished from the dawn of time.

June 1921

* * *

Today is the feast of Our Lady
Of Smolensk and clouds of blue incense
Drift over the grass, intermingled
With music more radiant than sorrowful.
And rosy-cheeked widows are bringing
Their sons and daughters to the cemetery
To pray at the graves of their fathers
—To the cemetery, this grove full of nightingales,
Now becalmed in the early morning sunshine.
And we bore to Our Lady of Smolensk,
We bore to God's Holy Mother,
We bore in a coffin of silver,
Our sun, extinguished by suffering,
Alexander, our immaculate swan.

August 1921

Three Poems

1

Oh yes, I loved them, those intimate gatherings, late at night:
Arranged on the little table, the glasses which gleamed like ice,
Drifting from steaming cups, the coffee's subtle perfume,
The wintery warmth of the fire-place pervading all the room,
The caustic jokes, the gossip, the casual chat about books,
And, promising friendship   or more, perhaps   that first
    uncertain look.

2

That wasn't temptation—temptation is rather something which waits
In silence to trouble the priest, to oppress the fasting saint,
Which, like a stricken eagle, can be heard to languidly scream
At midnight, in May, disturbing the novice's youthful dreams;
But elegant sinners like these—how could they understand
The law they never knew—the iron grasp of its hand.

3

Is it because I've left my frivolous ways behind,
That the sight of sombre palaces starts to trouble my mind?
Having grown used to the sound of church bells, lofty and pure,
And subject to laws more stern than those which bind us down here,
Already I find myself drawn to that fateful place
Of penance and shame, which all who are guilty of sin must face.
And I see the bright city, I hear the voice, so gentle and kind,
As if the mysterious tomb hasn't yet opened wide;
And there, all day, all night, through heat and cold, I'll wait
With head bowed down, to hear the judge pronounce my fate.

January 1917

New Year's Ballad

From high among dreary clouds, the moon
Filled the room with a muted light;
The table is laid for six—but only
Five are present tonight.

My friends, my husband and I have gathered
To greet the New Year with a toast;
But why do my fingers seem stained with blood
And the wine, like poison, burn in my throat?

Then our host, self-important and solemn, proclaimed,
Raising his glass in his hand:
'Let's drink to this country in which we all live,
Let's drink to our native land!'

And my friend all at once turned towards me and gazed
At my face, having just recalled
Who knows what, and exclaimed: 'Let's drink to her songs
Which mean so much to us all!'

But, as if in response to my thoughts, a third
Who'd relinquished the world of light
Knowing nothing, proposed: 'Let's drink to the one
Who couldn't be with us tonight.'

1923

from *REED* (1924–1940)

I play on all five of them.

Pasternak

The Muse

Each night as I lie awake and await her arrival,
My very life is suspended, it seems, by a thread.
Honour, freedom, youth—what do they matter
When my longed-for guest is standing over my bed.

And now she's entered the room. And studying me carefully,
She draws aside her veil to allow me to see
Her face. And I ask: 'Was it you who dictated to Dante
Those pages from Hell?' And she answers: 'Yes, it was me.'

1924

Voronezh

To O.M.

The entire city is frozen—everything seems
To be covered in glass: the buildings, the trees, the snow.
Everywhere patterned sledges speed past erratically;
Along pavements sparkling like crystals I timidly go.

Above the statue of Peter soar poplars and ravens
And the sun-washed, pale green dome of the sky is filled
With a cloudy light, while echoes of famous victories,
Won by a mighty land still drift from the hills.

And all around the poplar trees are beginning
To resonate louder and louder, like glasses raised
By thousands of guests assembled at a wedding
To wish us peace and good health for the rest of our days.

In the room of the exiled poet the Muse
And terror stand guard, one by one.
Outside the night goes on and on
And morning never comes.

4 March 1936

Dante

Il mio bel San Giovanni.
—Dante

Even in death he didn't return to
Old Florence, the town where he once belonged.
This man who, departing, never looked back
—It's for him alone that I write this song.
Night, torchlight, the final embrace,
The wail of fate from beyond the walls;
Even from Hell he sent her his curses,
In heavenly bliss he still recalled
Her beauty—but, barefoot, holding a flickering
Candle, dressed in a penitent's gown,
He never returned to the streets of Florence,
His faithless, abject, beloved town.

17 August 1936

* * *

Wild honey smells of freedom, the scent
Of sunlight pervades the dust;
A maiden's mouth exhales violets, but gold
Doesn't smell of anything much.
Mignonettes suggest water, the fragrance of apples
Suffuses the thought of love;
But everyone has known throughout the ages
That blood only smells of blood.

And in vain the governor appointed
By Rome washed his hands in public
As the rabble howled all around him;
And in vain the Queen of Scotland
Attempted to rinse the crimson
Stains from her slender fingers
In the sultry gloom of the palace.

1933

The Willow

> *And a decrepit cluster of trees.*
> —Pushkin

I grew up in a fragrant nursery, in beautiful stillness,
In a youthful age which had only just commenced.
And although I never cared for the voices of people,
The voice of the wind to me made perfect sense.
Nettles I loved and the burdock's vigorous growth,
But the silvery willow is what I loved the most.
And, who knows, in gratitude, maybe, her whole life long
She stayed beside me, shading me with her weeping
Branches, fanning with soothing dreams my sleepless
Nights. But how strange that she's died, while I carry on.
All that remains is this stump. Now other willows
Speak of something or other beneath the same skies—
Ours and yet different—speak in a foreign language;
But I remain silent, as though a close friend has died.

18 January 1940

* * *

When someone dies all his portraits
Undergo a subtle transformation.
The look in his eye changes
And the smile on his lips is different.
I noticed this once, coming back from
The funeral of a certain poet.
Since then I've tested my conjecture
Many times, and it's always confirmed.

21 May 1940

* * *

Thus sombre souls take wing and wander
Away… 'Pay no heed if I start to meander.

You arrived unannounced, without aim or design,
Unconnected with any particular time.

But stay a bit longer. Do you, by chance,
Remember we visited Poland once?

Our first morning in Warsaw? Who are you, I wonder,
The second, perhaps, or the third?' 'No, the hundredth.'

'But your voice is the same as it was in the past.
You know, for years I'd hoped that at last

You'd return—but now all I feel is indifference.
There's nothing I need from our earthly existence:

Neither Homer's nor Dante's marvels. I'll wander
In the realms of bliss before very much longer;

And Enkidu's alive and Troy still exists
And everything's drowned in a fragrant mist.

To drowse in the willow's green shade would be best,
But the sound of that bell allows me no rest.

What is it? A flock coming home from the lea?
But my cheek still awaits the cool of the breeze;

Or the priest on his way to distribute his bounty?
But stars light the sky and night veils the mountain;

Or a summons calling the people together?'
'It's the bell which tolls for your last evening ever.'

1940

Mayakovsky in 1913

I never knew you at the height of your glory,
All I recall are the first faint rays
Of your dawn; and now I can tell the story
Of just one encounter from those distant days.
The lines of your powerful verse were filled with
Strange new voices we'd never heard…
And your youthful hands were never at rest as
You raised up a terrible scaffold in words.
After you'd touched it, nothing could ever
Remain what it was before that time,
All that you shattered stayed shattered forever,
Condemned by your thundering words to die.
Frequently lonely, so often troubled,
You rushed on ahead, unable to wait
To play your part in the joyful struggle
To which you knew you were called by fate.
Somewhere the roar of the flood was growing,
Outside the rainclouds angrily frowned,
As we heard you read your rebellious poems
And debate all night with the stormy town.
And an unknown name, a new reputation
Like lightening flashed round the stuffy hall;
And preserved to this day in the heart of the nation,
It echoes still like a warrior's call.

8-10 March 1940

from *SEVENTH BOOK* (1936-1964)

The seventh veil of mist fell,
The one which is followed by Spring.

T.K.

from Craft Secrets

1

I've got no time for epic wars or
The sterile charms of elegiac conceits.
Everything in verse should be slightly out of order,
And not, as with people, excessively neat.

If only you knew what rubbish a poem
Can start from—for poems aren't fussy whence
They spring: the yellow of dandelions growing
With goosefoot and burdock by a wooden fence;

The scent of tar, mysterious cries in
The night, a patch of mould on a wall…
And already, slowly, the poem is arising,
Tender, impassioned, a joy for us all.

9 November 1936

6

Last Poem

There's the one which stirs like the thunder's din
And, breathless with life, comes bustling in;
It circles and lights on the tip of your tongue;
Then, laughing, it claps its hands for fun.

Another comes to me, who knows from where,
In the stillness of midnight it's suddenly there;
It looks at me out of the mirror's depths
And says something serious under its breath.

And some are like this: amid the glare
Of day, without seeming to notice I'm here,

Across a sheet of white paper it pours
Like a crystal stream through a mountain gorge.

And there's this kind, too: it wanders around,
It isn't a colour, it isn't a sound;
It takes shape, it changes, it twists and it writhes
And refuses to let you catch it alive.

Or this one: it sucks the last drop of your blood
Like a cruel girl who demands all your love;
Then without even feeling the need to explain,
It lapses into silence again.

But no pain is harsher than this, I suspect:
Winding tracks can be seen to stretch
Into the distance, remote, without limit;
It's gone… Yet without it, I know that I'm finished.

1 December 1959
Leningrad

from In the Year 1940

2

To the Londoners

Time is composing the twenty fourth drama
Of Shakespeare today with a steady hand.
Ourselves the guests at a terrible banquet,
Now we'll be able to understand
The story of Caesar, of Lear and Hamlet
As we hear them speak above rivers of lead.
With torchlight and song we'll follow our dear
Juliet right down to the scene of her death;
Through the window, secretly trembling with fear,
We'll spy on Macbeth and enter the hall
With the cruel assassin, hired for pay.
Only this one, the last one of all,
We don't have the strength to read today!

1940

from The Wind of War

3

The First Long-range Bombardment of Leningrad

Then one day, on the bustling streets,
Everything suddenly changed;
But whether in country or town,
Such a sound seemed equally strange.
In truth, it was somewhat akin
To the distant thunder's din;
But the rumble of thunder contains
A hint of moist clouds high above
And, delighting the thirsty green plains,
News of the rains which they love.
But this was a sound, hot and dry,
Which disturbed my ears as they tried
To deny what they couldn't ignore—
That each day it continued to draw
Closer, to spread and increase,
Threatening to casually unleash
On my son the destruction of war.

September 1941

7

To the memory of my neighbour, Valya Smirnov, a little boy from Leningrad

i

In the garden the trenches
Have all been dug.
Orphans of Petersburg,
Little children I love!
It's hard to breath underground,
When pain grips your head like a vice;

Through the bombs which are falling all round
I hear a child's quiet voice.

    ii

Knock with your little fist and I'll open
The door, as I used to do.
Today I live beyond deserts and mountains,
But I'll always stay faithful to you…
I never heard you complain
Or ask for a crust of bread.
Now bring me a branch of maple or bring
Some blades of grass, as you did last Spring;
Or bring me a tremulous palmful of plain,
Cold water, scooped from the Neva's flood;
And with it I'll wash from your golden head
Every last trace of blood.

23 April 1942
Tashkent

from Three Poems

2

As you rummage around in the shadows of memory
You'll find a pair of long gloves which reach
To your elbows, a Petersburg night and a scent
In the dark of a theatre, sultry and sweet.

A breeze from the bay. And ignoring the ohs
And ahs from the stalls, in a pause between lines,
He'll smile towards you disdainfully—Blok,
The tenor who sang of our own tragic times.

1960(?)

Sketches from Komarovo

Oh, Muse of tears.
—Marina Tsvetaeva

I've withdrawn from all prospect of happiness here,
I've renounced all earthly goods;
The spirit which guards this place inhabits
A fallen tree in the wood.

Life is no more than a habit—like guests
We've come for just a few days;
And I seem to hear two voices conversing
Up there in the aerial ways.

Only two? In a thicket of raspberry bushes
By the eastern wall I can see
A dark green branch of elder. A letter,
Perhaps, from Marina to me?

19-20 November 1961
The Harbour (in hospital)

from Poem Without a Hero

Part Three

Epilogue

> *May this place be deserted…*
> *—?*

> *And the desolate, silent squares on which*
> *Men were punished till daybreak.*
> *—Annensky*

> *I love you, Peter's creation.*
> *—Pushkin*

A White night on 24 June 1943. The city is in ruins. From the Harbour to the Smolny everything is clearly visible. Here and there persistent fires are slowly burning down. In the garden of the Sheremetov Palace the linden trees are in leaf and a nightingale is singing. On the third floor (in front of which stands a crippled maple tree) a window has been smashed in, and behind it yawns a black void. From the direction of Kronstadt can be heard the crash of heavy guns. But elsewhere all is quiet. The voice of the author, seven thousand kilometres away, speaks:

And so under the roof of the Fountain House
Where evening wearily wanders
With her lamp and her keys on a ring,
I answer the distant echo,
Disturbing with misplaced laughter
The impregnable slumber of things;
And the ancient maple which witnesses
Everything, looks through my window,
Extending its black, withered hand,
As though offering to help, at sunset
And daybreak, foreseeing the moment
When I'll part with my native land.
But the earth was rumbling beneath me

And a certain star looked into
This home to which I'm still bound,
Awaiting the signal agreed upon…
It's over there in Tobruk or
It's somewhere here that it's found.
(What revenge do you have in store for me,
You who have heard my bright ravings
—Though you're neither the first nor the last?
You won't drink deep—you'll just sip from
This anguish—the news that the moment
Of farewell is approaching fast.
Don't place your hand on my forehead
But bring to a standstill for ever
The time which your clocks proclaim.
Unhappiness won't overlook us,
The cry of the cuckoo won't echo
In our forests consumed by flame…)

And, lost in the heart of the taiga,
Behind fences of barbed wire
—Who knows what year we are in?—
My double's become a handful
Of dust, a story from history
And his trial is about to begin.
And now the trial has ended
And the Noseless Harlot's two envoys
Have been charged by fate to preserve
His life. And it's surely a miracle
That even from here the sound of
My voice is distinctly heard:

I paid them ready money
To keep you free;
For ten long years a revolver
Was aimed at me;
I wandered on, too fearful
To look around;
Behind me rustle glory's
Impoverished sounds.

…But you didn't become my burial-place,
My dear, disgraced, rebel city,
You grew pale, became speechless, appalled.
Our parting is only apparent,
How could I ever leave you?
My shadow is cast on your walls,
Your canals mirror back my reflection,
My footsteps are heard in the Hermitage
Where my friend and I once roamed,
Or else in the Volkovo Cemetery
Where I'm able to weep in freedom
By the graves of the dear ones I've known.
My verse has freed its wings from
All that was said in the First Part
About passion, betrayal and love;
Like eyes which are covered by heavy
Tombstones, my sleepless city,
Your windows are all boarded up…
And it seemed that you followed behind me,
But you stayed to die in the gleam of
The spire, the canal's mirrored lights;
You waited in vain for good tidings…
Now nothing remains above you
But the dance of your precious White Nights.
The happy word 'home' is forgotten
And like so many others I look through
A window which isn't mine;
In Tashkent or in New York City
The air which the exile breathes is
As bitter as poisoned wine.
But how you would all have admired me
As I sat in the flying fish's
Belly and fled from the spite
Of the foe above occupied forests,
Like the witches who fly on their broomsticks
To the Brocken on Walpurgis Night.

'Quo vadis?', someone enquired

As somewhere ahead the Kama
Was imprisoned in frozen bounds;
But before I could answer, the Urals
With all its tunnels and bridges,
Like a madman, began to resound.
And in front of me stretched that highway
Along which so many, including
My son, in the past have gone;
And across the Siberian landscape's
Solemn and crystal-clear silence
The road to the grave wandered on;
And, troubled by mortal terror
At a country reduced to ruins,
Yet already foreseeing the time
Of revenge: with dry eyes and wringing
Her hands in anguish, Russia
Journeyed east, and I followed behind.

Completed in Tashkent
18 August 1942

REQUIEM

Unmoved by the glamour of alien skies,
By asylum in faraway cities, I
Chose to remain with my people: where
Catastrophe led them, I was there.

    1961

In the terrible years of the Yezhov terror I spent seventeen months queuing outside the prisons of Leningrad. On one occasion someone 'recognised' me. It was a woman who was standing near me in the queue, with lips of a bluish colour, and who, of course, had never before heard my name. And now, waking from that state of numbness which was characteristic of us all, she quietly asked me (for everyone spoke in a whisper in those days):
'And can you write about this?'
And I replied:
'I can.'
And then something like a smile flickered across what was once her face.

1 April 1957
Leningrad

Dedication

Mountains are known to bend beneath such sorrow
And mighty rivers to cease to run;
But the prison doors will still stand firm tomorrow,
And behind them the cells will still resemble burrows,
And sadness will long for death to come.
For some cool breezes blow as day is dawning,
Others rejoice in sunsets—but here
Our days are all alike, monotonous, boring:
The hateful grating of keys on locks each morning
And the tramp of boots is all we can hear.
We arose at dawn, as if to pray together;
Through the ravaged city we made our way;
And the morning sun was low in the sky, the Neva
Was veiled in mist as, paler than ghosts, we gathered
And the sound of hope seemed so far away.
The sentence falls… She feels the tears searing
Her eyes, and now she's all alone;
And they'll cast her down, their fingers tearing
The life from her heart, coarse and uncaring;
But she'll stagger on down her lonely road…
We were thrown together in hell—and yet still I miss them,
Those random friends; and I wonder where they are:
What memories crowd the bright full moon, what visions
Haunt them now in their cold Siberian prison?
And I send this farewell greeting from afar.

March 1940

Introduction

This was a time when the corpses
All smiled, as though glad to have died,
When the city, reduced to an adjunct
Of its prisons, looked on from the side;
When driven half-crazy by suffering,
The ranks of condemned shuffled by
And the trains on the point of departure
Whistled a song of goodbye.
The star of death glimmered wanly,
Far below an innocent land
Was trampled by blood-stained jackboots
And crushed beneath black prison vans.

1

They took you as day was dawning,
Like a mourner I followed behind,
In the hallway the children were bawling,
The icon light guttered and died.
I'll never forget: when you kissed me—
The chill of your lips; on your brow—
Cold sweat. Now like wives throughout history,
I'll stand by the Kremlin and howl.

Autumn 1935
Moscow

2

Quietly flows the quiet Don,
The yellow moon, strolling along,

Enters a house without a care
And chances upon a shadow there.

Not long ago that shadow was still
A woman—but now she's lonely and ill.

Her husband is dead, her son is in jail.
Remember her in your prayers without fail.

   3

No, this isn't me, this is someone else who is suffering.
I wouldn't be able to do it—but let what has happened
Be veiled in black cloth, let the lamps be removed…
And then night.

   4

If only you'd known, wicked woman
Who once cared for nothing but fun,
Who used to be Petersburg's favourite,
That the day will finally come
When, along with three hundred others,
Clutching your parcel, you'll go
To wait in line while your tears
Burn through the New Year's snow.
The poplar tree sways near the prison
In silence—but so many lives
Are ending inside for no reason…

   5

At the feet of the cruel hangman,
Prostrating myself, I've groaned—
For seventeen months, my terror,
My son, I've called you back home.
Everything's muddled forever,
To me it's no longer clear
Who's a beast, who's a human being,

And whether the end is near.
And incense and blossoming flowers
And tracks on a road leading nowhere
Are all that remain… From the sky
A huge star looks into my eyes
And I finally understand
That destruction is close at hand.

1939

    6

The weeks flutter by on light wings;
What's happened—I scarcely can say:
How the white summer nights looked in
Through the bars of the cell where you lay,
How still they look down on you there
With the pitiless eyes of a hawk
While the voices of strangers talk
Of death and the cross which you bear.

1939

    7

The Sentence

And I felt the heavy verdict,
So long anticipated, fall
On my living breast. No matter,
I'll manage somehow. After all,

I've so many chores to attend to:
I must turn my heart into stone,
I must liquidate all my memories
And learn how to live alone.

And if not… Through my window summer
Is celebrating somewhere out of sight.
I've foreseen it: this house, so empty,
On this day, so desolate and bright.

Summer 1939

    8

To Death

You'll come one day for certain—then why not now?
Life is so hard; and while I wait, I've dimmed
The light and left the door ajar to allow
You in your simple splendour to enter in.
Assume for this purpose whichever guise you like:
Burst in like a shell with its load of death;
Sneak in like a skilful burglar as midnight strikes,
Or kill me like typhus, inhaled with a breath.
Or tell once more the well-known story we all
Have heard so often by now it's grown stale,
In which the men in military caps will call
And make the janitor's face turn pale.
To me it makes no difference. Quietly flows
The Yenisey. The North Star shines above.
All I can do is watch as terror enfolds
In mist those bright blue eyes I loved.

19 August 1939
The Fountain House

    9

I'm drunk on the harsh wine of madness
And all but concealed beneath
Its wing; and now it invites me
To enter the valley of death.

And I knew that I had to acknowledge
Defeat: that now it was time
To obey these delirious ravings
As if they weren't even mine.

And it won't allow me to carry
Any of my memories away,
However I try to persuade it,
Whatever I do or say:

Not the eyes of my son, filled with terror—
His suffering as adamant as fate,
Nor the day of the storm's arrival,
Nor the vigil at the prison gate,

Nor the hands' seductive coolness,
Nor the restless shadow of the lime,
Nor the sound of words offering comfort
From afar for one last time.

4 May 1940
The Fountain House

    10

Crucifixion

    1

Don't weep for me, Mother,
As I lie in my grave.

Choirs of angels hymned the glorious hour,
Dissolved in flame, the heavens glowed overhead.
'Why hast thou forsaken me, my Father?'
And 'Mother, do not weep for me,' he said.

    2

Magdalen sobbed and wrung her hands in anguish,
The disciple whom he loved was still as stone.
But no one dared to look toward the place where
The Mother stood in silence, all alone.

1940–43

Epilogue 1

I learned how to read the meaning of downcast faces,
To notice the way in which terror furtively peeks
From beneath half-lowered lids, how suffering traces
Its stern cuneiform script on ravaged cheeks,
How the hair which only the day before appeared
Lustrously black, can turn ashen grey overnight,
How smiles can fade on trembling lips, how jeers,
However dry, can betray a tremor of fright.
And if I now venture to offer up this prayer,
It's not for myself alone, but rather for all
Who, enduring the changing weather, stood with me there,
Beneath the indifferent gaze of that blank red wall.

Epilogue 2

Once more the hour of remembrance draws near
And it's almost as though I can see them all here:

The one who queued to the point of collapse,
And the one whose time on this earth has now passed,

And the one, who shaking her head, used to groan:
'When I enter this place, it's like coming back home!'

And I would have recorded you all in my verse,
But they've taken the list where your names were preserved.

So instead I've made you a shawl out of words,
Saved from the talk which I once overheard.

And I'll never forget you, wherever I go,
Whatever new horrors I'm destined to know.

And even if one day they somehow suppress
My voice through which millions of lives were expressed,

I ask that you all still remember to pray
For my soul on the eve of my burial day.

And if in the future they give the command
To raise up a statue to me in this land,

I consent to this honour—but only so long
As they solemnly pledge not to place it upon

The shore of the sea by which I was born,
For my link with the sea has long since been torn;

Nor in the park of the Tsars, by the tree
Where a restless soul is still searching for me;

But to raise it instead near the prison's locked door
Where I waited for three hundred hours and more.

For I fear I'll forget in the vacuous peace
Of the grave that old woman who howled like a beast,

Or the rumbling wheels of the black prison vans,
Or the sound of the hateful jail door when it slammed.

And from motionless eyelids the melting snow,
Like tears, down my cheeks of bronze will flow

As the dove in the watchtower calls from on high
And the boats on the Neva go drifting on by.

The Fountain House,
March 1940

Notes

Page 15. The epigraph to *Evening* is taken from the poem 'La vigne en fleur' by the French poet André Theuriet (1833–1907).

Page 21. From: *In Tsarskoe Selo*
Tsarskoe Selo was the name of a small town located 24 kilometres to the south of Saint Petersburg. It originally grew up around the summer palace which was named after Catherine, the second wife of Peter the Great, and which was largely designed in the mid-18th century by the Italian architect Bartolomeo Francesco Rastrelli. Also located in Tsarskoe Selo is the Alexander Palace, built for Tsar Alexander 1 later in the 18th century. In 1937 the town was re-named Pushkin, in memory of the poet, who was a student of its celebrated imperial lycée.

Page 26. '*Three Things…*'
The subject of this poem is Akhmatova's first husband, the poet Nikolay Gumilev (1886–1921).

Page 28. 'Imitation of I.F. Annensky'
Innokenty Fedorovich Annensky (1855–1909) was a poet and director of the lycée at Tsarskoe Selo, where Akhmatova's family lived after leaving Odesa. Annensky's poetry exercised a profound influence on the members of the Acmeist literary group.

Page 29. The epigraph to *Rosary* is taken from the poem 'Justification' by Evgeny Baratynsky (1800–1844).

Page 35. 'The voice of Memory'
Olga Afanasyeva Glebova-Sudeykina (1885–1945) was an actress, singer and dancer. Akhmatova first became acquainted with her in 1913 and they remained friends until Glebova-Sudeykina went into exile in 1924. Lines 7-8 refer to the suicide of the poet Vsevolod Knyazev (see note on 'Poem without a Hero', Page 90).

Page 36. '8 November 1913'
The probable addressee of the poem is the poet and translator Mikhail Lozinsky (1886–1955). Lozinsky was a life-long friend of Akhmatova.

Page 38. 'I came to visit the poet'
The poem is dedicated to Aleksandr Blok (1880–1921), one of the leading Russian poets in the early years of the 20th century. Towards the end of his life Blok lived at 57 Dekabristov Street in Saint Petersburg, close to the mouth of the River Neva.

Page 39. The epigraph to *White Flock* is taken from the poem 'Dear One' by Innokenty Annensky (see note on 'Imitation of I.F. Annensky', Page 28).

Page 43. 'God shows no mercy…'
The 'Chinese pavilion' mentioned in stanza 3, line 3, is to be found in the park surrounding the Catherine Palace in Tsarskoe Selo (see note to 'In Tsarskoe Selo', Page 21).

Page 45. 'July 1914'
This cycle of two poems was written shortly before the outbreak of war between Russia and Germany on 1 August 1914. The third stanza of poem 1 includes an allusion to the Gospel of Matthew, 24, 7, in which Jesus prophesies the end of the world. The final stanza of the second poem contains an allusion to the Gospel of Mark, 15, 24: 'And when they crucified him, they parted his garments, casting lots upon them, what every man should take.'

Page 47. 'Solace'
The epigraph is taken from chapter 9 of a narrative poem entitled *Mik* by Akhmatova's first husband Nikolay Gumilev, who served as a front-line soldier during World War 1 (see note to 'Three Things', Page 26).

Page 50. 'I'll draw out from the depths…'
This poem was dedicated to the artist Boris Anrep (1883–1969), whom Akhmatova met in 1915. After his departure from Russia in 1917 Anrep settled in Great Britain where, among his other achievements, he created the mosaics which decorate the stairs of the entrance to the National Gallery in London.

Page 53. The epigraph to 'Plantain' is taken from the poem 'Poltava' by Aleksandr Pushkin (1799–1837).

Page 55. 'When on his far-away island…'
Another poem dedicated to Boris Anrep (see note to 'I'll draw out from the depths…', P.50).

Page 59. The epigraph to 'Anno Domini' is taken from the poem 'I knew her even then…' by Fyodor Tyutchev (1803–1873).

Page 61. 'I wasn't one of those…'
Some commentators have detected in the second stanza an allusion to the prophecy of Dante's exile spoken by his ancestor Cacciaguida in *La Divina Commedia, Paradiso,* XVII, Lines 58-60:

> 'Tu proverai sì come sa di sale
> lo pane altrui, e come è duro calle
> lo scendere e'l salir per l'altrui scale.'

(You will discover how salty is the taste/Of another's bread, and how hard it is to go down/And ascend another's stairs.)

See also the note to 'Dante', Page 73.

Page 62. 'Lot's Wife'
The poem is based on the Old Testament story of Lot's wife (Genesis 19, 15-26). When God decided to destroy the city of Sodom in punishment for its wickedness, he agreed to spare Lot and his family on condition that they refrain from looking back as they flee from the city. Lot's wife, however, was unable to resist the temptation and was turned into a pillar of salt.

Page 64. 'Everything's plundered…'
The poem is dedicated to Natalya Rykova (1897–1928), a close friend of Akhmatova.

Page 65. 'Today is the feast of Our Lady…'
Aleksandr Blok was buried in the Smolensk Cemetery in Saint Petersburg on 10th August 1921 (see note on 'I came to visit the poet…', Page 38).

Page 69. The epigraph to 'Reed' is taken from the poem 'Improvisation' by Boris Pasternak (1890–1960).

Page 72. 'Voronezh'
The poem is dedicated to Osip Mandelstam (1891–1938), whom Akhmatova visited in 1936 during his exile in Voronezh. A statue of Peter the Great stands in a public square in the centre of the city.

Page 73. 'Dante'
Akhmatova was a passionate admirer of the poetry of Dante (1265–1321) and knew many passages from *La Divina Commedia* by heart. The epigraph is derived from *Inferno*, Canto 19, line 17.

Page 74. 'Wild Honey'
In the second stanza the governor appointed by Rome is Pontius Pilate, the governor of Judaea, who, according to the Gospel of Matthew in the New Testament, absolved himself of responsibility for the death of Jesus by washing his hands. The Queen of Scotland is Lady Macbeth, who in Shakespeare's play obsessively tries to wash her hands of the blood of King Duncan after his murder.

Page 75. 'The Willow'
The epigraph is taken from the poem 'Tsarskoe Selo', written in 1823 by Aleksandr Pushkin (see note on the epigraph to 'Plantain', Page 53).

Page 77. 'Thus sombre souls…'
Enkidu is the name of a character from the ancient epic poem *Gilgamesh*.

Page 78. 'Mayakovsky in 1913'
Vladimir Mayakovsky (1893–1930) was one of the most celebrated Russian poets of the early 20th century. In his early career he was associated with the Futurist movement and after the October Revolution he became closely involved with the Soviet regime. He committed suicide in 1930.

Page 79. The epigraph to 'Seventh Book' is taken from the poem 'The ice-floes split and the frosts ring out…' by Akhmatova's friend, Tatyana Kazanskaya (1916–1989).

Page 83. 'To the Londoners'
The poem was occasioned by reports of the bombing of London by the German Luftwaffe during the Second World War.

Page 84. 'The First Long-range bombardment of Leningrad'
Akhmatova was resident in Leningrad during the first days of the siege of the city by the German army. She was later evacuated by plane to Moscow, and from there to Tashkent in Uzbekistan (see note on 'Poem without a Hero', Page 88).

Page 86. *From:* 'Three Poems'
For information on Aleksandr Blok, see note on 'I came to visit the poet' (Page 38).

Page 87. 'Sketches from Komarovo'
Marina Tsvetaeva (1892–1941) had committed suicide shortly after her return to the Soviet Union from exile in Paris. The epigraph is taken from Tsvetaeva's cycle of poems *Verses to Akhmatova*, written in 1916.

Pages 88-91. 'Poem without a Hero'
'Poem without a Hero' is a long poem in three parts. In Part 1 the lyrical heroine looks back on her life in Saint Petersburg from the vantage point of Leningrad in the early 1940s. The Epilogue constitutes Part Three of the poem and is set in Leningrad during the siege by the invading German army.

Page 88. The first epigraph taken from words attributed to the Tsaritsa Yevdokiya Lopukhina, the first wife of Peter the Great who, according to popular legend, after she was forced to enter a convent, placed a curse on Saint Petersburg, the

Tsar's new capital city. The second epigraph is taken from the poem 'Petersburg', by Innokenty Annensky (see note on page 16). The third epigraph is taken from 'The Bronze Horseman', a poem by Aleksandr Pushkin (see note on page 53).

Page 88. 'A White Night on 24 June 1942…'
The Sheremetov Palace, also known as the House of Fountains, was built on the banks of the Fontanka river in 1750 as the Petersburg residence of the aristocratic Sheremetov family. In the latter part of her life Akhmatova lived in a flat located in the palace. In September 1941, at the start of the German siege, Akhmatova was evacuated from Leningrad to Moscow, and in autumn 1942 she was again evacuated from Moscow to Tashkent, the capital city of the Soviet republic of Uzbekistan (see note on page 84).

Page 89. 'It's over there in Tobruk or…'
Tobruk is a city on the coast of Libya which was occupied by Axis forces during the Second World War. In November 1942 it was recaptured by an allied army.

Page 89. 'And the Noseless Harlot's two envoys…'
The significance of the image of the 'Noseless Harlot' remains uncertain—but most commentators are agreed that it probably represents death.

Page 90. 'All that was said in the First Part…'
At the beginning of Part 1 of 'Poem without a Hero' the lyrical heroine finds herself in the mirrored hall of the Sheremetov Palace on New Year's Eve 1940. Here she is visited by the phantoms of her friends from pre-revolutionary Petersburg. Dressed for a masquerade on New Year's Eve 1913, her former companions evoke a romantic entanglement in which a young poet commits suicide after his lover has left him for a rival. This melodrama echoes the suicide of Vsevolod Knyazev in response to the relationship of Olga Glebova-Sudeykina with the poet Aleksandr Blok (see note on 'The Voice of Memory', Page 35 and 'I came to visit the poet…', Page 38).

Page 90. 'Quo vadis?…'
The phrase 'Quo vadis?' means 'where are you going?' in Latin. According to popular myth, this was the question put to Christ by the apostle Peter when they met in the course of Peter's flight from Rome in the period after the crucifixion. The phrase served as the title of a novel published in 1896 by the Polish author Henryk Sienkiewicz.

Page 91. 'Along which so many, including/My son…'
Akhmatova's son, Lev Gumilev, endured successive periods of imprisonment in labour camps between 1938 and 1956. Akhmatova's experience of her son's arrest is the subject of several poems from the cycle 'Requiem'.

Pages 92-100. *Requiem*
Requiem 1 was written on the occasion of the arrest of Akhmatova's husband, Nikolay Punin, in 1935, at the start of Stalin's Great Terror. Other poems in the cycle commemorate the arrest and sentencing of her son, Lev (see the note to *Poem without a Hero,* Page 91).

Page 99. *Requiem, Epilogue 1*
The 'red wall' referred to in the final line belongs to the Kresty Prison in Leningrad, where Akhmatova visited her son in the days following his arrest.